Three A. M. at the Museum

Poems by

Alarie Tennille

Cover design by Chris Purcell

Cover: *Triptychon Shared Loneliness II* by 4th Life Photography,
file #73503660, licensed from Adobe Stock

ISBN: 978-1-954353-60-2

Kelsay Books
502 South 1040 East, A-119
American Fork, Utah, 84003

Acknowledgments

*inspiration: an asterisk before the word "inspiration" indicates that curious readers can find the artwork that inspired the poem accompanied by the poem at *The Ekphrastic Review* (ekphrastic.net) or look at the art by googling the title and artist.

With warm appreciation to the following publications where these poems first appeared:

Allegro Poetry Review: "At the Window," "Reigning Cats"
Black Dirt Review: "After Hurricane Florence"
Deep South Magazine: "Alone at the Diner," "Moving On"
Dying Dahlia: "Switching on the Light"
Ink, Sweat, and Tears: "Aunt Vera and Uncle…"
KC Poetry on the Move Competition 2019: The three cinquains collected under "Kansas City Eats" were finalists, published separately on posters placed at the downtown trolley stops and on the trolleys.
Minute Magazine: "Breathing in the Sea," "Taking Forever One Day at a Time"
MockingHeart Review: "Leave a Message at the Tone"
Night Garden Journal: "The Witch Turns"
Rusty Truck: "Evening News"
Silver Birch Press: "The Caregiver," "How to Become a Werewolf"
The Ekphrastic Review: "A Dead Tolima Woman Speaks to Her Dead Husband," "All-Night Diner," "Angel of Showing Up," "At the Movies with Monet," "Brainstorms," "Christina Olson," "Commute," "Entering Pollock's *Enchanted Forest,*" "Ghost Town, Population: 1," "Instead of going to the beach we go see Mrs. Joy," *"Le Temps Perdu,"* "My Ancestors Send Me Dreams," "Night Watch," "Open House," "Party for Two," "Pharmacy of Forgotten Cures, Balms, Purges, and Sundries," "Playing Dominoes on the Homefront, 1943," "Procession in Fog," "Reading the Signs," "Remorse," "René Magritte: *The*

Unexpected Answer," "Rothko," "Sea Change," "Self-Portrait in Quarantine," "Shivering in the Church Yard," "Soup Is Forgiving," "Waiting," "War," "Women in Black," "When Stars Outnumbered Streetlights"

The I-70 Review: "Full-Moon Singing Bowls," "Franz Marc: *The Large Blue Horses,*" "Giving Nothing Its Due," *"When the pupil is ready, the teacher will come"*

Tipton Poetry Journal: "Mama Kept Her Secret"

Verse-Virtual: "Because I Misread 'Cow' for 'Crow,'" "Justice for All"

Wild Goose Poetry Review: "Dear Toaster," "Poetry 101"

Special Thanks

Many thanks to everyone who has encouraged and supported my poetry. I wish I could name all of you. Special thanks to:

• Karen Kelsay (Kelsay Books/Aldrich Press) for publishing *Running Counterclockwise,* which was a finalist for the 2015 Thorpe Menn Award for Literary Excellence, and *Waking on the Moon* (2017).

• O.P.W. Fredericks and Daniel Milbo (The Lives You Touch Publications) for publishing my chapbook, *Spiraling into Control,* which launched me into the poetry world.

• Tammy Daniel for proofreading my manuscript and critiquing poems at my request.

• George Bilgere, Melissa Fite-Johnson, and Al Ortolani for writing blurbs for this book.

• Lorette C. Luzajic of *The Ekphrastic Review* for publishing so many poems in this collection, for writing the Foreword, "Fantastic Ekphrastic," for nominating "War" for the Best of Net 2020, and for awarding me the first Fantastic Ekphrastic editor's choice award in 2020.

• Artist friends Richard Eric Disney and Michael Driggs for agreeing to submit their artwork to *The Ekphrastic Review* to accompany my poems.

• My treasured critique group members, Tina Hacker and Teresa Leggard, who help make me the best poet I know how to be and keep raising the high bar.

• My husband, Chris Purcell, for his patience in living with a night owl, his support, design advice, and expert proofreading.

Finally, I want to thank The Writers Place, for continuing to make Kansas City a great home for writers.

Fantastic Ekphrastic

I have felt very fortunate, at the helm of *The Ekphrastic Review,* to have the unexpected gift of Alarie Tennille. Alarie has been a regular contributor of gorgeous ekphrastic poetry from the early days of the journal.

As if that wasn't gift enough to an editor, I have also been most grateful for her generous, unwavering support, whether through advice, insights, ideas, or cheerleading on our behalf. There were times I wondered what I had gotten myself into, undertaking responsibilities for a literary journal that has grown into a landmark and destination for the ekphrastic genre and its community. Alarie felt like a guiding light to me at times when things got messy or overwhelming. Knowing that the journal means something to writers of her stature is no small thing. In fact, it kept me going to know that a writer of Alarie's talent was reading her fellow poets every day and working on her next ekphrastic contribution to submit.

Alarie has been integral to the Ekphrastic family from the start, and in addition to her faithful reading and ongoing submissions, she has offered her astute observatory powers and her expertise as a prize nomination consultant and a guest editor on several occasions. She has shared our journal far and wide so that her colleagues would have a broad audience. Honouring her with our first Fantastic Ekphrastic editor's choice award was a no-brainer, in recognition of her ekphrastic excellence and her impact on our literary journal.

The gift of Alarie is not exclusive to *The Ekphrastic Review:* Alarie is a treasure to the ekphrastic world and the literary world in general. Here is her work for all of us to have and to hold and cherish.

Alarie's poetry holds the unique ability to open our eyes in new directions and catch what we might miss. She observes the ordinary long enough to find its magic and show us, too. The poet Al Ortolani noticed this, and said, "Tennille is a master of the subtle bump, the tap on the shoulder—the hey, look again." This captures the essence of her poetry, and indeed, the essence of what poetry should be: accessible and enchanted at the same time.

Alarie's talent for finding the right words and arranging them in a way that encourages us to look closer holds within it yet another special gift. Her passion for art runs parallel to her powers of observation and her keen insights into the stuff of everyday life and people, and she sees in paintings and sculptures the same mix of simple and complex themes, the same array of ordinary and transcendent moments.

Her poetry finds the face and the heart of an artwork, and it takes us by the hand to show us, too. Just as often, she opens a doorway to an unexpected layer, and shows us how to look for the moments we may have missed, the part of art that exists on the sidelines or in the background. The poet Leonard Cohen's muse, Suzanne, comes to mind, when she shows you how to look "among the garbage and the flowers."

Alarie has an uncanny tendency to step into the shoes of every passerby and every painting. Sometimes it is only for a moment, and other times for that proverbial mile, but she takes us with her every step of the way.

Through her art, we experience art more vividly, and feel more deeply the interior lives of those around us. From blue horses to breakfast eggs to the evening news, Alarie's poetry teaches us to pay attention.

Lorette C. Luzajic
Founder and Editor, *The Ekphrastic Review*

Contents

Some of us just know we're living in the wrong time, place,
or body.

The cells of your body will echo in harmony with the moon—
om om om om.

*Staring up at the stars, I gaze into the past—where my childhood
    memories still dance beyond the moon.*

*Aha moments arrive like lightning bolts just as you'd expect
    from firing neurons.*

*...when the mist
between the subconscious
and waking mind thins.*

Three A.M. at the Museum

This is the time when the mist
between the subconscious and waking mind
thins. The art becomes more receptive
when it can speak to us one-on-one.

To enhance your communion with art, we insist
on no talking. You will visit each gallery alone.
Security guards will try to make themselves
invisible.

Silence your inner critic and listen
with your eyes. We recommend spending
at least ten minutes with a work you might
normally hurry past.

Walk back and forth as you study the art.
Do eyes follow you?
Even if there are no eyes?

Imagine you can climb into the canvas
and look out. What sounds do you hear?
Do you feel warm or cold? Feel eager
to run away?

Stop at a portrait and imagine yourself
as that person, waiting for someone like you
to visit. Or count how many colors you find
in an Impressionist sky.

Silently invite the art to tell you its secrets.
If you visit the Ancient Egyptian gallery, stay
as long as you dare.

Rothko

*inspiration: *Untitled (Black on Red)* by Mark Rothko (1957)

"Untitled"—an invitation
to share, collaborate, decide
what this art means, how it feels—
at least on this day—
at least to you.

Or maybe a dare.

It worked. You stopped,
not like the Don't Get It rushing by,
afraid of any syncopation
in the status quo.

Wrap yourself in hot red.
Shiver against prickles of icy blue.
Afraid to look at what lurks
in the dark or ready to throw
open the window? Perhaps
the blurred edges remind you
of your fading life.

So what if you're still confused?
Something has shifted.
You've begun to talk back.

*inspiration: an asterisk before the word "inspiration" indicates that curious readers can find the poem with the artwork that inspired it at *The Ekphrasti* *Review* (ekphrastic.net) or look at the art by googling the title and artist.

Night Watch

*inspiration: *Two Women with Cat* by Omar Odeh (2011)

At 3:00 a.m., two eyes stare
in my window, floating impossibly high
above the ground. *Your own reflection,*

I tell myself without believing—
one pupil open wide to gather
the light, the other a pinprick.

Night, the thief of color, plunders
peace, smothers the calming melody
of birds and white noise of traffic,

signals the mind's stray mutterings
to move in. Ideas I've hidden
even from myself skitter

across the page, trying to escape
surveillance. Tomorrow I'll discover
a message in a mysterious hand

left on my desk. I jump at a yowl—
a neighbor's cat in the alley—
but the eyes peering in never blink.

All-Night Diner

*inspiration: *Nighthawks* by Edward Hopper (1942)

The Help

Every night the same. Six months
slogging by like ten years. Rarely see
five customers after ten o'clock,
but I need to pay tuition. Sure hope
the war ends before I finish college.

But tonight, when the bell tinkles,
sunshine pours in the door.
            Va-va-va-voom!
Can't take my eyes off the redhead.
Neither can Midnight Joe, my regular.
Can't sleep when his son's on a ship
God-knows-where.

What's with her date? He doesn't
look at her at all. Won't say a word.
Just holds up his cup when he wants
a refill. She deserves better.

Redhead

What a creep! Guess I don't like
the strong, silent type after all.
He seemed nice enough
at intermission when he asked
me out for coffee.

Smiled when he told me he spotted
me from the balcony. With hair
like a neon sign, I hear that a lot.
Soon there won't be any bachelors
around older than this blond kid.

We chatted about the concert
till we got here. Then he clammed up
like he thought I might be a spy.
Maybe he's one.

Joe

I know what the kid's thinking.
Look at him drooling over the dame.
She's a class act, but that guy with her
is either an idiot or deploying—
still an idiot. You need to grab
a life while you can.

Silent Man

I'm an idiot. One look and I
was a goner. Can't look at her now.
Tomorrow I leave for boot camp.
Won't burden her with that.

Giving Nothing Its Due

Here's to white space, to pregnant
pauses, to the hole-punched backdrop
of polka dots, to the dancing room
air leaves for snowflakes.

Here's to the breath
between notes that changes sirens
to music, to the moment after
a good book, symphony, kiss.

Here's to dull diary days, to sips
of water between courses,
to small talk before we take
the stage.

Let's applaud Nothing
for giving Something
our full attention.

At the Window

inspiration: *At the Window,* oil painting by Richard Edward Miller at Nelson-Atkins Museum of Art, Kansas City

Encaved in the chill of the museum,
I forget time. Can't tell the hour
or season in the programmed winter
dusk. Entering this gallery, I catch
light pouring in the open window,
smell the garden's invitation
to step outside.

A woman already stands at the sill.
Sheathed in a meadow of silk,
she leans into the breeze,
closes her eyes. I can feel the sun
on her face just as she must feel
the artist's gaze. She steels
herself to stay with her guests
in the parlor. Like me, she must
wait for spring.

Remorse

*inspiration: Untitled by Bahman Mohassess (1990)

He'd heard that no disaster
in a nightmare could actually kill you.
But how did anyone really know?
And why couldn't he remember
that comforting fact till he exploded
from sleep?

Tonight his psyche worked
overtime. Two mugs of warm milk
couldn't stop his shivers, erase
the sight of the weird, amorphous
creature that ran him down. He'd faced
gorier, scarier assassins than this
humanoid storm cloud.

Normally, he'd wake up
when a monster grabbed him.
No such luck. The blob plunged
its fist deep in his gut, pulled
its hand out dripping with blood.

He didn't scream, faint, or wake,
just stood gawking at his assailant.
The blob clutched its side like *it* felt
the pain—its mouth an O of horror.
It reminded him of that time Dad
took a belt to him for breaking
the neighbor's patio door. He'd never
forget that *what have I done?* expression—
how Dad looked more shattered
than the glass.

26

Entering Pollock's *Enchanted Forest*

*inspiration: *Enchanted Forest* by Jackson Pollock (1947)

Resist the urge to run. Don't be
deceived by the lack of fresh air
and pine. Push past the brambles,
sit against a tree, and wait.

Forests only pretend
to be empty. Feel the ground
trembling, hear your imagination
cawing overhead. Horses gallop
through, then a bison escaped
from the caves of Lascaux.
Do not fear the Cossack.
He wants to play his accordion
for you, nothing more.

Keep going and you may come
across my father, looking amused
that you found him.

Soup Is Forgiving

*inspiration: *White Soup Bowl* by Anne Vallayer-Coster (1771)

Not enough salt or chicken?
Soup forgives the mistake.
A little too much? That's never
a problem at our house.

Maman says I'll have to wait
till I'm older to bake bread.
Because we can't eat bricks,
says Michel.

But YOU can go weed the garden,
she tells him, swatting him with
a towel. She winks at me—just us
girls now.

Soup, soup, soup every day—
if we're lucky. I don't think Maman
forgives Papa for dying. No more
Sunday roasts. She cries a lot.

The butcher saves soup bones
for us. Other neighbors help
when they can, but no one
has extra.

Cupping her hand, Maman
shows *this much salt to start.*
You can always add more later.
(I know better than to waste.)

I add a bay leaf, thyme, and bones
to the kettle of water while she chops.
It will take hours. I'm hungry
already, but don't say.

My tummy rumbles. She puts
a finger to her lips and hands me
a small chunk of bread. *Papa
would be proud of you.*

Time shuts its door, keeps us
from knowing the future, the future
from knowing us.

A Dead Tolima Woman Speaks to Her Shaman Husband

*inspiration: gold breastplate, Middle-Period, Pre-Colombian, Tolima Region, 1 B.C. to 700 A. D.

Time shuts its door, keeps us
from knowing the future, the future
from knowing us. Only after passing

can I see the ghost-colored men
who will assault Tolima, dig
through the dust of our children's

children's children. They will find
many treasures, but not the truth.
Your gold breastplate, born of the sun,

will wink at them. *Here lies
a leader, a man of power,* they
will think, just as I did when the glint

off your chest first pierced my heart.
A warrior, they will say, never
understanding our people prefer

making music to bearing arms
or that the power in your hands
was healing. What will they think

of me? Nothing. Like countless
women before me, I leave the world,
and history will speak not a word.

My Ancestors Send Me Dreams

*inspiration: postcard sketch, *Tower of Blue Horses* by Franz Marc (1913)

I am a tribe of one—
my own elder,
my own shaman,
my own voice chanting nonstop
in the cave of my skull.

For four nights, four horses
have gathered on the horizon,
painted blue by dusk,
untroubled by any idea
of Apocalypse.

North, South, East, West—
standing together, a towering
totem, all looking toward me.

Maybe they'll come back
tomorrow and tomorrow
until we are one.

Shivering in the Church Yard

*inspiration: *The Blue Church, Prescott* by Prudence Howard (1933)

His
tombstone
cast
a long
shadow,
stretching
from
his
death
toward
hers.
She began skipping
church, afraid to watch
his reach growing
shorter.

Procession in Fog

*inspiration: *Procession in Fog* by Ernst Ferdinand Oehme (1828)

Squeezed out by the heavy feet
of mourners, an unearthly fog
rises from hell. Day after day, the dead
pass my door, followed like a shadow
by those who can still pray or dig.

I think I see Mother,
and she's been gone ten years.

Death, like a new pastor, busily
makes the rounds to every household
before winter.

I have nothing more to say to God
for myself, but ask mercy for parents
who plead, *Please, Lord, please.*
Take me instead.

I Have a Certain Reputation

*inspiration: *Salomé* by Henri Regnault (1870)

I hear your whispers: *Salome the Slut,*
Princess Prostitute, Prophet Slayer.

Despite what you've heard,
I had no sinister plan
before my famous dance.
A hundred times a day, I go back
to that evening, feel all eyes caressing
my body, know I can win some treasure
with undulating hips
        and scarves that follow my curves.

I begin slowly,
    theatrical foreplay,
        use my graceful arms to say,
                "Come touch me."

I twirl and spin—

    faster,

    faster,

until Herod swoons, drunk with desire.

Women have no say
without using wealthy, powerful men.
My lewd stepfather revolts me.

I spot my turns a foot above his head.
He fancies I'm looking dreamy-eyed
at him, but it's the Baptist's eyes I see,
looking straight through me

to a dark place. I know he's locked
in a cell below.

Herod offered me a reward.
Mother chose John's head.
I got the blame.

I believe the Baptist knew
exactly what was coming.

Le Temps Perdu

*inspiration: *Rainy Night at Étaples* by William Edouard Scott (1912)

Strange to think of such a night
as paradise, even in memory.
A piercing, cold rain moved in—
not uncommon for a fishing village—
just one more reason to leave.

My wet shawl shuddered, my numb
feet shuffled on. Swinging wide to avoid
the corner puddle—*almost home, almost
home*—I stopped. The swirling water
shimmered under the lamp post
as though posing for Monsieur Monet.

Glancing up, I saw the daffodil windows
of home, glowing like a light house.
Was Maman expecting a guest?
As I reached for the handle,
the door swung in. I swooned
in the warm fragrance of *coq au vin.*

Maman wrapped me in a blanket
by the fire, rubbed my feet dry.
Did I even thank her? All day long
I'd been daydreaming of life in Paris.
Pourquoi?

On that night, before the Great War,
Étaples was perfect. Now no place
feels like home.

Christina Olson

*inspiration: *Christina Olson* by Andrew Wyeth (1947)

History dropped me here in Maine.
My forebears fled the shame
of Salem. Cut family ties
to the so-called Justice who hanged
women like me—those who don't blend
in, who speak their minds, only bow
their heads from a noose.

They say one of those witches
cursed our line with her last
breath. If so, that curse waited
for me. My twisted legs have thrown
me to the ground so many times
they refuse to carry me anymore.

My body wasn't suited to a life
of pumping water, building fires—
my limp arms almost as useless
as my legs, scarred by burns
from heavy cast iron skillets.

Daddy didn't want a school teacher
looking down on him, demanded I stay
home and help mother. Said I was smart
enough for a girl. Another kind
of crippling.

I see the looks of pity. *Poor
Christina, scrabbling just to hang
onto that weathered house,
near useless land.*

They'll never know the peace I feel
when I sit in this doorway and cast
my thoughts far, far out to sea.

Forty Years Later, Miss Dorothea Remembers
Sunday School Picnics of the Depression

Lord, it was hot! But that never stopped us
from cramming into Ebenezer Baptist
on Sunday morning. Men looking fine
in they suits. Ladies in they hats and dresses.
We just left the door standing wide open
and fanned ourselves with those paddles
from the funeral home. Looked like a hundred
butterflies with Jesus on their wings
'bout to lift us to heaven. Once we got
to swaying with the choir, we forgot the heat.

But we didn't forget all that food calling
us to grace. Sweet tea and Miss Addie's special
lemonade. A deacon tipped a flask to make
it even more special. We turned a Baptist-blind
eye to that! Fried chicken and potato salad
and a whole wagon of watermelon. Course,
it was always a competition for best pie.

We witnessed our own parable
of the loaves and fishes, the way plates
got filled four or five times for those who'd go
hungriest the rest of the week.

Playing Dominoes on the Homefront, 1943

*inspiration: *The Domino Players* by Horace Pippin (1943)

Happy clatter: click and clack—
dominoes in white and black—
we hunger for a chance to win
at anything (and there's no sin
in that).

What's it matter? Click and clack—
White folks win, and we're still Black.
But, even as we share their war,
we hold a hope worth living for.
Amen.

The Old World shattered, we want rights—
the freedoms now reserved for whites.
For don't our men miss kids and wives
and dare to sacrifice their lives?
They do.

For now, we chatter. Click and clack,
playing games till peace comes back,
while Mama quilts more steadfast seams
to tuck around the fervent dreams
we share.

War

*inspiration: *Potato Theatre* by Toyen (1941)

At the outset, we say
we'll be brave, we say
we'll survive. We promise
ourselves quick victory
like we're playing at the World Cup.

But it's never Us vs. Them.
Fear, grief, hatred, and hunger
attack from within. In a few
months, I'll do anything.
ANYTHING
for a bowl of soup,
loaf of bread, safe bed.

Every day I hear boots on the stair,
bombs whistling overhead—
hallucinations. I'm drowning
in my imagination.

I'm afraid to look in the mirror,
suspect I'll see both body and soul
already split apart and waving
surrender.

At the Movies with Monet

*inspiration: the film, *I, Claude Monet,* at the Tivoli in Kansas City

Naturally, we go to an art house.
Monet remembers the first movies
by the Lumière brothers. I assure
him his art will be shown in full color.

It's almost dark, nearly quiet
fifteen minutes before the show.
Few couples chat, preferring to sit
side-by-side staring at their private
mini-screens. No one notices Monet.

He jiggles my seat, nervous
without a smoke. *Mon dieu!* he says.
Relax, you'll be great, I promise.
Pffew! he adds. *I despise the opinions
of the press and the so-called critics.*
I tell him he coined the motto of our times.

A loud ringtone at the end of our aisle
makes him jump. *Sacré bleu!* he explodes.
When a woman's voice over speaker phone
tells us she's had an upsetting day,
Claude leaps to his feet.

I tug hard on his famous tweed jacket,
make him sit. We're both relieved
when Bergman's Death appears
on screen in his black cloak, warning us
to turn off cell phones.

A few minutes into the film, Claude
pulls out his handkerchief. It's him,
all him in his own words, voiced
by an actor who gradually shifts his voice
to the crackle of an old man. *I don't sound
that old,* Claude grumbles.

First we see the caricatures he was
selling at age fifteen when he met Boudin.
He watched the well-known painter
at work, capturing the dazzling sunlight
on women with parasols and frothy dresses
enjoying a day at the beach.

Magnifique, Claude whispers.
Remembering the man who inspired him
to paint outdoors for the rest of his life,
he wipes his eyes.

Open House

*inspiration: *White Doors* by Vilhelm Hammershoi (1905)

Can't you imagine coming home
to this stately gem each night?
I let clients think I opened every single
door to let in light and show off
the stunning woodwork. *Well below*
market price—the owner took a job
overseas. For sale AS IS, so you can add
your personal touches.

Last night I closed each door. Today
they gaped wide open. *As you wish,*
I whispered. I'm leaving well enough
alone, afraid to do my morning walk
through.

A ribbon of cold air trails me, room
to room. I brought my collie, still leashed
to the porch rail—as far as she'd come.
Crossing my fingers this place sells today.
I'll lower my commission if I have to.

Can't you feel the history? I ask
the young couple, giving them my card.

Aunt Vera and Uncle…

Half a picture, half a story.
I didn't know my uncle's face
or even his name—
he was Vera's Mistake,
Vera's Good for Nothing,
the mysterious Him of family legend.
And though I often wanted
to snip my brother
out of family photos,
I was made to understand
that no wrong,
no amount of ornery meanness
would ever equal
what this uncle by marriage
had done to us all.

Reading the Signs

*inspiration: *The Best Is Yet to Be* by Lorette C. Luzajic

BAM! STRIKE! Get ready for it.
Your fate is about to change.
That's right, I don't use tarot cards

or read palms. I read faces, and yours
is calling my bluff. So why can't you
believe the best is yet to come?

First you must run toward it, work for it.
Go out and search for hope. Carry
a butterfly net into the fog of despair.

Blindly scoop if that's the best you can
do. Unseen forces will guide you.
It's much like the work of a poet

looking for ideas. Here's a poem, there's
another. What signs do you track?
Like dreams and fingerprints,

the numbers, symbols, and sounds
that you sense will be unique to you.
But many clients report a feeling

of weightlessness, like they're floating
out of a dense gray fog into a cobalt
blue sky, with splashes of neon sunrise.

Some of us just know we're living in the wrong time, place, or body.

Sea Change

*inspiration: *Beyond the Storm* by Dale Patterson (2019)

Never expected the flying fish
to take to the sky. So many centuries
of evolution—building fin strength,
growing auxiliary lungs.

Have they adapted to escape
the oil spills, the tons of plastic
choking the sea? Or did they follow
the example of those first whales
who strode on four legs
into the waves to stay?

Across miles and years, the sea
calls me back. I chose the right day
to return. Some of us just know we're living
in the wrong time, place, or body.

Self-Portrait in Quarantine

*inspiration: *Figure* by Guillermo Wiedermann (1959)

Day 20-something: can you believe
I'm growing paler? The raised-by-wolves
hairdo isn't helping either, so I'm avoiding
mirrors. Instead, I'll look inward, paint
a self-portrait.

I try cubism: no need to change
out of jammies or examine my face.
Replace my head with an open book—
a nod to realism. No arms or legs since
I'm frozen in time.

My heart flattened into a greeting card,
my torso a dressmaker's form, parts of me
wired together with coat hangers.
My third eye wanders to my gut
and stares back without blinking.

Commute

*inspiration: *18th Street East* by Michael Driggs (contemporary)

Who hasn't thought it?
You're driving home
through the gray part
of town, in the gray part
of day. Almost sleepdriving,
following other cars
in an ant trail
up and down,
up and down—
the red lights barely bright enough to break
your trance.

What if—just once—
you take off, turn onto the interstate.
St. Louis, Chicago, Denver—
commit to a direction and go!

The Witch Turns

Go back! You think I can't hear
you swishing through the grass
for the fierce wind—the very wind

I conjured from screams of women
left broken by your kind. Sarah
Good, Rebecca Nurse, Susannah Martin—

those poor innocents proved by death
they were not witches. Never
will I stand trial. Never.

Your stench stalks me like a shadow.
So be it. Even without trees or ravines
for cover, we're secluded. I, too,

am counting on that. Closer, closer,
closer you come, never guessing
this very ground is under my spell.

Nothing can touch me here. Nothing.
You'll learn soon enough.
I half turn, cast my one-eyed curse.

You smirk just like the others.
I say nothing, for your kind cannot hear.
One step closer—a shriek of wind

your last memory.

Ghost Town, Population: 1

*inspiration: *Noe Valley* by Matthew Rackham Barnes (1943)

Haven't seen another soul
in six months. Does that make
me a ghost? Do ghosts know
they are ghosts?

Don't see any cars either.
It's impossible to get a cab—
but I can't really complain.
Some of us prefer our own
company.

The neighborhood suits me—
cheap rent, peaceful. Perfect
for a writer, though living here
does kind of mess with my head.

Am I dreaming?
That would explain the half-baked
reality: lights, but no street signs,
no sounds, not even wind or rain.

Maybe heaven and hell
are the same place.

Here They Come!

While humans are quarantined,
penguins get their first tour
of The Nelson-Atkins Museum of Art.

Tiny tourists in tuxedos burst
into the galleries.

The paintings look down from their frames,
silently chuckling. They miss visitors
as much as these new Friends of Art,
who gawk back at them
with equal wonder.

The zoo guests prove to be
discerning critics. Water lilies?
Not part of their habitat.
But John the Baptist?
Him they can relate to.

Caravaggio captures the fatigue
of a tired dad, trying to keep up
with toddlers. Drooping in the heat,
he sits slumped, splayed legs,
happy to stay right there,
watching them for hours.

Waiting

*inspiration: *Spatial Concept: Waiting* by Lucio Fontano (1963)

I dress like an extrovert—
red silk—my smooth second skin. Love
its illusion of power, wealth,
all the confidence I lack.
But I feel the rip—
deep, hidden clawing
from the inside out.

My therapist nods.

Waits.

The silence swallows me.

Go on. Name your demon.
What are you doing about it?
Why have you taken so long?

Waits.

Do you think you're the only one
living in fear? No one is born
with self-understanding.

I shiver.

Don't you know that waiting
is the worst thing you can do?

How to Become a Werewolf

Do you ever have insomnia?
Experience disturbing dreams
at the full moon? Then you may be

ready for an exciting change!
It's easier than you think. That's
right, for just $39.95 plus shipping

you can get our glow-in-the dark
instructional booklet and DVD (for rainy
night viewing). Sure, you could search

for a werewolf to bite you, but just think
how many ways that can go wrong!
Like violent death, duh. Our patented

DYI process has proved safe and effective
for a smooth transition. Why wait to explore
your wild side? You can start tonight!

That's right, warm-up nocturnal exercises
will accelerate your training. Stay up till 1:00,
2:00, even better 3:00 a.m. (You don't want

anyone around to ask what you're doing,
do you?) Keep it a surprise! Your improved
night vision will be a plus in step 8: Learning

to Stalk through Dead Leaves. Call NOW …
Operators are standing by during the hours
of darkness in every time zone. Warning:

Avoid watching horror films. They'll only
confuse you. You must find your own darkness.
Listen to those strange voices you don't think

are you. They really are. We all have good reasons
to sing at the moon, to excavate the caverns
of our minds. Progress is remarkable.

By week six, most report accelerated hair growth,
a break in the voice, a craving for rare meat.
Consult your doctor if you develop persistent

homicidal thoughts. Symptoms may vary.
So how will you know you're a werewolf?
Like falling in love, you'll just know.

René Magritte: *The Unexpected Answer*

*inspiration: *The Unexpected Answer* by René Magritte (1933)

Later you will wonder
how I locked the bedroom door
from the inside. "Open up!"
you'll yell. Try the knob, barge
in without an answer.

For the rest of my days,
I'll relish imagining that moment
you find the room stripped,
empty as your heart.

After Hurricane Florence

Flying north from Atlanta
to Richmond, we're spared
glimpses of Wilmington, now
an island, and the roofs
of Florence, not spared by her
namesake, trying to tread water.
Yet all the rivers, running red
with clay, spill out of their banks—
like bloody, clawing fingers,
like countless ruptured arteries.
We turn away from warnings
that the Earth
is bleeding out.

Winter Bares Its Teeth

Outside the study window, winter
camouflages almost as well as summer
leaves: gray bark, gray sky, dingy snow,
the window screen and poor vision adding
another layer of gray.

Yet I catch some motion, a hulking
form, a bluer gray larger than a squirrel,
and something alarmingly red. *A hawk,*
says my husband, rushing for the camera.
I saw a bloody feather on the porch—
maybe a robin.

Outdoor creatures know an arctic blast
barrels our way. At least the small bird
will be spared that agony. Until now,
predator and prey both busy filling
their bellies for tomorrow.

I see the majestic head bend and rise,
bend and rise, as the raw mound
at his feet grows redder.

Sprung

We are, after all, only human.
Don't hear daffodil stalks
trumpeting through the earth,
don't vibrate to the squeal of
melting ice. Can't smell
the tom next door swaggering
by, claiming he owns us.

We need stronger proof
of spring: bursts of color,
Easter sales, a tax deadline.

When our new cat bolts
out the door, we wonder
how he could be so blind
to the comforts of home.

Justice for All

Over 200 prospective jurors
swell the room. Good Americans.
The court clerk praises us for coming.

Congratulations for stepping up—
for filing behind our military on the front
line of valor. She applauds us

for keeping our streets safe, helping
our neighbors as we might one day
need help. A filmstrip validates

how we are upholding our Constitution,
preserving our freedom and justice.
Now who here feels that jury duty

poses an extreme hardship?
Half the room forms a line
to leave.

Ever Wonder What It's Like to Be a Book?

You picture us as sage tribal elders
unable to share what we know
unless asked. Just sitting here waiting,
waiting, waiting—longing to save humans
from repeating the same mistakes—
like book burning.

Perhaps you see us as puppies alone
in our shelter cages, lacking moist eyes
and thumping tails to plead *Pick me! Pick me!*
You imagine we yearn to be taken home,
cradled in your arms. Not really.

Ever wonder how we feel about you?
Of course not. Exactly my point.
Comrades from used bookstores send word
of broken spines, torn pages. Scribbling!

What about subjecting us to forced labor—
holding up table legs, letting in a window's
breeze, then forgetting us when it rains?
You're very good at forgetting us—
on buses, in hotel rooms.

But I can sense your empathy, can tell you
are an avid reader. At least you're still listening,
so I'll level with you. What we love most
is pressing close to each other, trading
our stories, histories, and skills with the book
next door.

Home libraries are the best. On public shelves,
I'm too likely to stand between my clones.
Save me from myself, and I'll do
the same for you.

The cells of your body will echo
in harmony with the moon—
om om om om.

Full-Moon Singing Bowls

In the Himalayas,
where time moves
almost as slowly as the mountains
and ears lean closer
to the heavens, natives continue
a legacy of 2500 years.

Full moon sings crescendo
and craftsmen catch the notes,
strong arms working in harmony
to lasso lunar power.

A half moon, shaped from the seven
sacred metals, glows red at the forge:
time to break the silence of night.
The percussion of many hammers
pounding in turn, like well-timed pistons.

Bang turn *bang* turn *bang*—
a cratered bowl emerges, a hollowed-out
moon, turned upward to capture night
song. Each bowl taught to sing one note
of the seven chakras.

Close your eyes to polished beauty
and choose by sound. Find the frequency
that speaks to you. One *clang*—
then run a mallet around the rim
the way you'd play a crystal goblet
with a wet fingertip.

Now fill the bowl with water. Watch it
reach a cool boil, send silver bubbles
dancing across the surface, leaping
like dolphins into the air.

The cells of your body will echo
in harmony with the moon—
om om om om.

Franz Marc: *The Large Blue Horses*

*inspiration: *The Large Blue Horses* by Franz Marc (1911)

A trinity of wild horses,
heads curled down in devotion,
contemplate their wholeness,
their power, their shared cloud
of warm breath. They have
no Mondays.

Day canters by, and they exult
      in the wind, running east along the rise, then turning
            and heading elsewhere
      as though tugged by invisible reins, propelled
                by sure purpose.

The sun pauses on the horizon
as they trade colors with the mountains,
shedding red chestnut for nightfall blue.
Bellies full of sweet grass, they pay
homage to stillness.

Watching, we feel our breathing slow.

The Caregiver

I'm wearing a mask
like I'm part of the medical team.

For the second time
in three days,
I'm sitting on a gurney,
watching my blood pressure creep up, up, up
on a monitor
as I'm prepped
for surgery. Try taking
deep breaths.
No help.

Then she arrives
with her *I'm here for you* smile
and reassuring hand on my arm.
"Would you like a warm blanket?"

Nothing short of waving a magic wand
could be better. Why must operating
rooms be icy? She tucks me in.

In my mind, she's the same nurse
who went through the same steps
48 hours ago, but I know she isn't.
Slowly and clearly she explains
what will happen next. Asks,
"Any questions?"

She sees me—
an intelligent human being,
a rational adult who minutes ago

felt like a weepy five-year-old,
but who now wants to show
this mom surrogate
how brave I can be.

Taking Forever One Day at a Time

I love

the way you return from errands
with a present—a Danish, book, or bottle
of champagne

how you thank me for every meal
from *coq au vin* to a ham sandwich
and make coworkers think
I'm Julia Child

hearing your voice in conversation
downstairs before realizing
that you're talking to the cats
in the same serious tone you use
with plumbers

how you told me I was funny long before
anyone else did

that time in France when I said our waiter
looked like Orlando Bloom and you answered
then we'll have to come back tomorrow

the fun of reading a book you've just finished
and finding *oops! duh!* or *what a jerk!*
penciled in the margin

the way you reach for my hand
before crossing the street

how you describe every dark-eyed
brunette—*she looks like you*—no matter
how silver I go.

No wonder forty years have sneaked by.

When the pupil is ready, the teacher will come.

—Chinese proverb

Before showing us any moves,
our tai chi instructor lectures
for forty-five minutes. *Good chi enter
head. Bad chi leave through feet.*

I grow stiff on philosophy, but perk
up with his warning that cats steal
our chi. It's especially dangerous
when they sleep on our pillows—

no wonder I'm too tired to concentrate.
Cats are hotter than humans,
and apparently I am the power outlet
for three purring radiators, twelve feet

to clean of negative energy as they stomp
around my lap. I'd welcome a sunny
windowsill about now. Picture my three
cats awaiting my return. I'm ready

to copy their Zen state. Finally!
We are invited to stand, raise our arms
overhead, and sink our chi. I look around
at clumsy humans. No one stretches

with feline elegance. No one can leap
six times his height. I'm dropping
this class and going home to study
the real masters.

Breathing in the Sea

*inspiration: *Wind from the Sea* by Andrew Wyeth (1947)

A visitor once ran from this room—
thought she saw a ghost. I admit
these frail lace curtains take on a life
of their own, but I believe people
carry their own ghosts with them.
Been here all my life and never
seen one.

Everything about this house is spectral
gray. New drapes would only make
the walls cry out for paint.
I'm content to live in the past.

The fluttering flowers and birds
are right pretty. Grandmother Hathorn
made them. Maybe she figured
they were as close as I'd ever come
to a bridal veil. We redo to make do
in this house.

Sometimes I take a nap up here,
watch the curtains billowing
until they lull me to sleep.
Don't they look frothy like seafoam?
Muslin would snap like sails.
The sea breathes right through
the lace.

Welcoming the Year of the Horse

at the Nelson-Atkins Museum of Art

Girls launch glowing yo-yos
twenty feet into the air while drums
throb encouragement. In another hall,
cymbals increase the pulse, egging
dragons to dance and flirt with the crowd.
Children squeal. Marble columns
and floors play ping-pong
with the clamor.

I escape to the Age of the Horse—
a period room from 1754 with calm
blue wainscoting—a room to myself
even though I can still hear the frenzy
below. I imagine the sound of needles
whispering to cloth, of silk slippers
rasping closer to the fire. I want
to pull up a chair.

"Everybody was Kung Fu fighting"
wafts through the fake sunlit windows.

Kansas City Eats

Out for Barbecue

Roadhouse—
harmonica
served with a side of ribs.
Music so loud it's like hot sauce
for ears.

Story: Best New Chef of 2014

Cuisine—
what we call food
when it seduces eyes
and makes a drooling mouth quiver
for more.

Foo's Frozen Custard

I'm not
the only one
making this my dinner—
line snaking out the doorway. No
complaints.

(These three cinquains were finalists in the 2019 KC Poetry on the Move
competition. Each was illustrated beautifully by Audrey Morrison before enjoying
its prize: riding the downtown trolley and advertising the wonders of Kansas City
to tourists.)

81

Alone at the Diner

Thinking coffee.
Thinking wheat toast thinly spread
with raspberry jam over a pond of butter.
Thinking two eggs, yolks running away,
corralled by a fence of bacon.
Thinking, "I'm the only customer,"
but feeling you lean across the table.
Knowing you want a taste.

Angel of Showing Up

*inspiration: *Angel of Showing Up* by Richard Eric Disney (contemporary)

Titles matter too much in your world.
Go ahead—laugh. I've had other positions.
Miracle Worker—now there's a title to impress.
Everyone loves a miracle. (Just so you know,
lottery money is not a miracle.)

Putting one foot in front of the other
can turn into a miracle. Everyone suffers
through days when they don't want
to get out of bed or leave the house, times
when they feel family or friends slipping away
and can't see that they are the ones
backing out the door.

Can't you remember when you moved
to a new school in third grade? How the kids
said you talked funny and had cooties?
How many times did you pretend you had
a stomach ache?

When did you last sit down to dinner
with your whole family?

The thing is. Some people ask for help
and some don't understand that they need it.
I just show up to observe and listen first.
I've got a blue bird on one shoulder and bunny
on the other. People seem to sense their vibes
before they see them.

Since you're talking to me, I know Bun
and Blue will materialize soon. Tell me
if you see something different. I may need
to call for backup.

Rozzelle Court

café at The Nelson-Atkins Museum of Art
Kansas City, Missouri

The Italianate cloister
invites us to a quiet lunch,
yet there seem to be more
echoes than people to make
them. Conversations strum
guitars. Children's voices
chirp like flutes. Notes
that should fly into the sky
bounce back from the climate-
controlled ceiling, ricochet
off the tiled floor.

We're nearly smothered
by a densely woven chord,
punctuated by plinks of fountain,
cymbals of dishes clashed on glass
table tops. The sound wraps over us
like a cowl, invites us to turn
inward.

Our eyes sense stillness
in the shadows, tamping
the cacophony, muffling
chatter and distraction
into a calm without quiet.
We are, at last, cloistered.

Chinese Landscape Scroll

A scouting party of white-gloved
curators went before you
savoring the pleasure, rolling
back time inch-by-inch.
They traveled east to west
for over a thousand years.
Now the full vista lies open—

    resist the rush.

Imagine you've slipped
on a long silk robe that dices
your steps. You arrive at cliff's edge.
Let the mist roll over you. Rest.
Meditate. Try to clear the whirr
of machinery from your ears,
the congestion of chatter
from your mind. You will fail,
of course. But walk slowly
through the mountains, pause
to drink in the waterfalls. Envy
the ancient travelers who stay
here forever. The more time
you take, the more ready
you will be to go back
to the beginning
and start again.

Staring up at the stars,
I gaze into the past—
where my childhood memories
still dance beyond the moon.

Women in Black

*inspiration: *Women in Black* by Marianne Von Werefkin (1910)

Staring up at the stars,
I gaze into the past—
where my childhood memories
still dance beyond the moon.

I never could see the shapes
astronomers join into constellations,
but I find patterns familiar to me.
On this cold night, the stars pull

me back to Russia, to the women
in black. I never could tell one
from another. To be honest, I didn't try.
Their sameness captivated me.

Whether 25 or 70, they shared
the same weary shoulders and dark
shrouds. Their symmetry of motion
turned washing clothes at the river

into a hypnotizing choreography.
I missed them in winter when the river
froze. By October, darkness would fall
before dinner. As the women

hurried home, they faded
into the sky. The white bundles
on their backs glowing like stars
as they passed our windows.

Instead of the beach we go see Mrs. Joy

*inspiration: *Alacena* by Maria Izquierdo (1942)

who's nearly 90 and lives alone
in a Victorian house, shaded by huge
magnolias. On the short drive, Mama
tells me Mrs. Joy is a character
who still climbs out on her roof to clean
her gutters. Truth be told, Mama
is a character, too.

The hall so quiet and dark
against the summer day—Persian rugs
swallow the sound of footfalls. *Tick-tock,*
tick-tock from the Grandfather clock in the hall
until we don't notice any more.

Mrs. Joy also has a spinet like the one
Thomas Jefferson owned, but it stays
quiet like her other furniture. She says
the tour guide at Monticello told her group
there were only two others like it
in the world and didn't believe she had one.

I stay tuned to their conversation
though I don't always get it. "Little pitchers
have big ears," says Mama. She says that a lot,
but never explains it. I can smell a pie
that's almost done.

Till then, I stand with arms clasped
behind my back—like I'm in a china shop,
even though all the treasures here are safe
behind glass. Right at eye level—close
enough for even me to see.

I marvel at the iridescent tea cups—
so much like shells I find at the beach,
the tiny fingers of the woman dancing
a minuet, the stiff ruffles that look
as sharp as coral. Fairies, angels,
and animals are the best! I almost
forget about the pie.

Moving On

Mr. Selby carved the S in the mantel,
planted the roses, laid the parquet,
but couldn't lay himself to rest.
Put so much into the house
it was a natural choice
for a second body
when his gave out.

"Come in, Mr. Selby!" we'd shout
at dinner when the heavy front door swung in.
He loved to smell Mama's cooking,
but would open cupboards looking
for something else to eat.

Not many families can name their ghosts,
but Mama woke one night to see him sitting
on the end of her bed, said she wasn't
frightened. To prove her theory, she asked
an elderly neighbor to describe Mr. Selby,
who had died only six years before my family
moved in.

We'd hear his tread on the stairs,
had to put latches on bedroom doors to keep them shut—
shut tight as my eyes, not wanting to see
even a friendly old man visiting my sleep.

Eventually we moved to a new house.
For a few years my family rested in peace.
Then the Selby house was bulldozed.
Stained glass and wainscoting buried.
Queen Anne passing away
beneath an apartment block.

That's when Mr. Selby joined us in the burbs.
By now he'd learned to dial the phone.
We wondered who was taking his calls.

Mama Kept Her Secret

As a child, Mama's chicken and dumplings
reminded me of "Diddle, diddle, dumpling,
my son John." That made me smile,
even though I resented the chicken
for not being fried.

When I got married, dumplings became
her peace-offering to my new husband.
On Sunday afternoons, we'd go over to do
laundry. Any reason to drop by Mama's
included dinner.

Chris cooed over the best dumplings
ever, then proved his praise
by polishing off the pan.

No one expected Mama's heart attack
at age 59. I didn't get her recipe before
our next Sundays stopped. Neither did
my brother.

A few years later, I hoped Maya Angelou's
cookbook would save me. Angelou added
carrots, celery, and onions, making her broth
even better. The chicken matched Mama's.

But those dumplings? More like heavy
clods of Arkansas clay than Mama's sea-breeze
dumplings from Georgia. We still miss
Mama's poetry on a plate.

Switching on the Light

I wake in the dark.
A man stands silhouetted
in the doorway. I try to scream,
find my voice sleep-paralyzed
like my legs.

Shhh, it's only a dream,
whispers my husband, pulling
me close. My moan fades.
My adrenalin soars.

I wake in the dark.
A man stands silhouetted
in the doorway. Repeat,
repeat. Over twenty years
of reruns.

I blame the serial rapist
who haunted college nights.
The one time my roommate
was gone, he climbed
through the window next door.
How can that other woman
ever sleep again?

At work the next day, I explain
to a friend why I'm dragging.
*This man in the dream
never speaks or comes
toward you?* she asks.

Maybe he's not an intruder.
When you were little,
didn't your daddy stand
at the door like that to check on you?

When Stars Outnumbered Streetlights

*inspiration: *Fin de la Jornada* by Emilio Boggio (1912)

River and road wind along,
side by side. River babbles.
Road keeps its bored silence.

Laborers slog home
before darkness fills
deep ruts, twists ankles,
costs a week's wages.

Downcast eyes and lives
seldom notice sunset shimmering
on the water. Just a few neighbors,
hypnotized by streaming light,
smile as they pick up the pace
for home.

In It to Win It

Family road trips—
a melted misery of togetherness. We stick to the seats, breathe
    the double chain-smokey air, and rumble and grumble along.
                At least the roads aren't so bumpy when we leave
Virginia.

Mama says it's time for the alphabet game
We call out a word as we see the next letter
                                                    whizzing by.
Amoco
                beach   company   delivery,
calls Geoff.

I'm looking for another Amoco station. Can't use the same
sign, even Quaker State,   6 seconds after my brother,
with his 5-year advantage in reading and 50-foot advantage in
vision.

Exit   fairgrounds   gas   hotel...
I can't see any license plates. Goodbye *X, Y, Z,*
                                not that I make it that far....

At 8 or 9, I get my first revenge.
Geoff has a chess set under his arm. He's just learning,
so we're rookies together.

He explains how each piece is allowed to move.
I win my first and only game. He packs up
the board without a word.

When I'm about 10, Mama worries
I'll soon turn into a giddy teen.
"Never ever LET a boy win," she warns.

Why would I ever do that?

*Aha moments
arrive like lightning bolts
just as you'd expect
from firing neurons.*

Brainstorms

*inspiration: *Hors du Cercle* by Joan Miro (1920)

*A survey in 2013 showed that 65% of Americans believe
humans use only 10% of our brains. From MRI technology,
we now know this is a myth.*
—MedicalNewsToday.com

Aha moments
arrive like lightning bolts
just as you'd expect from firing neurons.
Yet most thoughts bounce randomly by
like tumbleweeds or balls of yarn
batted out from under the sofa by a cat.
Only you don't knit.
Do you own a cat?

When you sleep,
your brain works overtime and expects
more genius from you. Sends messages
in Mandarin characters. Requires you
to interpret the calligraphy of ten blackbirds
perched on a power line. Hands you a mic
and pushes you on stage—only you don't know
the play, can't sing, and haven't prepared
for a TED Talk. You can't even explain
why Winnie-the-Pooh shows up
at sessions of Congress.

You need sleep for good health, so why
won't the brain dim the lights and hum
ommmm?

Poetry 101

Let's jump right into this. Please
take out some paper and write
a jellyfish.

You mean a poem? asks Ms. Front
of the Class. No, I never confuse
a jellyfish with a poem. Do you?

I mean make me see, feel, want
to be a jellyfish. Say I'm an alien
from Planet Xanax

or someone who's always lived
in the mountains of Tibet. Introduce
me to your jellyfish.

Maybe you can tell me why it's easy
to tell a jellyfish from a poem—
or why is that hard?

Because you can see through
a jellyfish to what lies behind it,
suggests Mr. Loves to Talk. *Like*

in a poem, he adds. *They move*
like they were spilled into the ocean,
suggests another guy in the back.

Ms. Worried says, *I've never seen*
a jellyfish. You're lucky, I say.
You can write the confessions

of an imaginary jellyfish. While talking,
my eyes go to the girl in the red cashmere
sweater and the guy who just rolled

out of bed. Both are writing furiously,
already out to deep sea,
not looking back.

Pharmacy of Forgotten Cures, Balms, Purgatives, and Sundries

*inspiration: *Pharmacy,* collage by Joseph Cornell (1942)

You'll find us tucked in a back alley, lost
in a maze of boarded-up shops. A few clients
insist we relocate between visits. Most find
one stop satisfactory.

The bell tinkles and I step out from the back
curtain. New patrons look confused, stopped
by the imposing oak counter, unlabeled
bottles out of reach.

They often wave a prescription, but we don't take
them. *What is bothering you?* I ask. They don't
always know, but I do.

They'd walk out if I said, *You've lost your
butterfly wings, banished your whoopee.
Spend two weeks in Sicily or write a book on fly
fishing.*

Our custom blends will let them find the cure
for themselves. You seem open to the unknown.
For you, I'll blend lapis, cinnabar, the last rosebud
of autumn, the first raindrop of spring, remnants
of Thursday night's dream.

I don't expect to see you again unless you
choose to be my successor.

Evening News

In Akron today, a cat pounced
at a flat-screen TV, knocking
two U.S. Olympic skiers off course
before being apprehended. Both
skiers have been airlifted
in critical condition, the gold
medal going to Norway. Details
at ten.

Congress called an emergency session.
This is an outrage that cannot continue,
a disgrace to our country. Constituents
are tired of senseless violence killing
dreams, stealing futures, say Senators
X, Y, and Z. *It's time to act.*

Sources have leaked proposals:
requiring background checks
on all cat owners or an outright ban
of indoor cats, a move endorsed
by the FTC. Conservatives call
for building a wall to keep cats
from infiltrating our borders.

Rest assured, say all respondents,
we'll do everything we can to keep
our young people safe. Rest assured,
assured, rest, safe, must keep ourselves
safe, safe, safe. Must do something.
Tomorrow, tomorrow, tomorrow.

Reigning Cats

They say you shouldn't keep
more cats than you have
rooms in your house,
though they probably mean
your average, 12 x 14 foot rooms.
Perhaps at Versailles
you could squeeze in a few more.

Cats playing tag and skidding
after balls down the Hall of Mirrors,
accepting as their due bowing
servants, curtained beds,
and a profusion of gold
reminiscent of their days
with the pharaohs.
Every strutting tom
would fancy himself the Sun King.

You might be able to house
a whole dynasty of cats
if they were allowed to roam
the grounds, willing to risk
the trick fountains
and clumsy feet
of bourgeois tourists.
Though, frankly, cats are not
so keen on *égalité* and *fraternité*
as we.

Leave a Message at the Tone

Sorry I missed your call.
I thought the ringing
was in my ears. Too busy
reading Tarot cards
for my cat and polishing
paper clips—no reflection
on you.

I also missed the Pulitzer
Prize, lifeline call
from Who Wants to Be
a Zillionaire, along with my
raison d'être, which may
be buried in the laundry
hamper, tucked
into a stray sock.

I'm not going to pretty up
the truth. Sometimes
I'm a turtle with my head
pulled into the shell,
a race car stuck in reverse,
a Moscow Mule
in a lead mug. Nowhere
does my résumé say
receptionist.

Because I Misread "Cow" for "Crow"

"Black cows wheeling overhead"
make me wonder *why?*
Returning to the constellation Taurus?
Fed up with the same patch of pasture?
Too bad those cows don't have lanterns
to flit about with the fireflies.

I should stop staring up
with my mouth open.

Still, I can't resist pondering *why?*
and even *why not?* Such mysteries
are common, thanks to Myopia,
my muse.

Dear Toaster,

You deserve a morning person,
someone who bounces out of bed
like, well…you know how you do.

I can't even look at your shiny
morning face without seeing
my sheet wrinkles, bed head,

and pre-coffee frown. I need to ease
into day with Debussy. You're
the cymbals in a Sousa march.

I'm the cat in a You Tube video
who falls off the counter
when you erupt.

Party for Two

*inspiration: *Reply to Red* by Yves Tanguy (1943)

Dad wanted a going away party. We
tried, but we do not eat, drink, dance,
or get jokes. *Party Poopers!* he said. We
do not poop either. But we yelled, *Clink!*
and wished him safe travel in 50 languages.

Every night we still toast Dad, our android
developer, even though he returned to Earth
183 days, 5 hours, 13 minutes, and 7 seconds ago.
We continue to transmit data, but suspect
our real mission was to keep Dad company.

He named us Floozie and Monk—
probably another joke we do not get.
Dad said if he had his laboratory here
Floozie would have red hair and we both
would have opposable thumbs. Human
vanity. We lack nothing.

At 1900 hours, we stop work. *Clink!*
I tell Floozie. *Welcome home, Monk,*
she says.

About the Author

Alarie Tennille was born and raised in Portsmouth, Virginia with a genius older brother destined for NASA, a ghost, and a yard full of cats. A Phi Beta Kappa, she graduated from the University of Virginia in the first class that admitted women (B.A. with distinction in English). She met her husband, graphic artist Chris Purcell, in college. She still misses the ocean but loves the writing community she's found in Kansas City.

After a career ranging from technical editor to greeting card writer, Alarie is retired and has more time to focus on her poetry writing. She serves on the Emeritus Board of The Writers Place. Previous publications include a chapbook, *Spiraling into Control,* and two poetry collections from Kelsay Books, Aldrich Press: *Running Counterclockwise* (2014), which was first runner-up for the Thorpe Menn Award for Literary Excellence, and *Waking on the Moon* (2017). Alarie won a 2020 Fantastic Ekphrastic Award from *The Ekphrastic Review* and has been nominated three times for a Pushcart Prize and twice for Best of Net. She has been published in numerous journals (see Acknowledgments) and anthologies. Alarie hopes you will visit her website and subscribe (free) to her blog at alariepoet.com.

Made in the USA
Columbia, SC
11 June 2021

39635429R00071